Tinfoil Hand-Cut Stars: Midwinter Poems and Musings

Jennifer Gurney

ISBN: 978-93-6354-544-1

First Edition: 2026
Rs. 200/-

Cyberwit.net
HIG 45 Kaushambi Kunj, Kalindipuram
Allahabad - 211011 (U.P.) India
http://www.cyberwit.net
Tel: +(91) 9415091004
E-mail: info@cyberwit.net

Printed at Repro India Limited.

Dedication

Tinfoil Hand-cut Stars: Midwinter Poems and Musings is dedicated to Beth Kempton. The poems and short pieces in this book were written during her Winter Writing Sanctuary late December 2025 - early January 2026. I have found Beth to be the single-best writing coach, inspiration, nurturer on the planet. This is the third year I have taken her Winter Writing Sanctuary and each year it gets better. Taking time at the darkest time of year to seek the light is a spectacular experience. I highly recommend it, as well as her course Words Heal, which I took shortly after Todd died. I experienced the class a second time a few months later and found it to be even more helpful then. Beth, thank you for offering such spectacular writing courses to help inspire us. I am so incredibly grateful to you.

Note: This year's Winter Writing Sanctuary was organized by color. I have organized my writing by day so that the poems inspired by a certain color can be read together.

Contents

1.1 Green - nature / evergreens / hope

A Study in Green

Green looks like:
Christmas tree, house plant, limes, cucumbers, broccoli, grass, moss, the sea, eyes, watermelon, honeydew, kiwi, Christmas tablecloth

Shades of green:
kelly, mint, lime, sea, loden

Green makes me think of:
Grandma Heitman's house - her bayberry candles were red but smelled like green to me

Green smells like:
Pine trees at Christmas time, but also when Todd and I used to ride the Harley in the mountains. There was that one stretch of highway when we'd turn left at the top of the canyon coming up from Boulder and we'd ride through the pines and it would smell so fresh and clean. It always made me cry, for some reason, I never knew why. And he had a hard time smelling things but could usually smell the pines. That made me happy.

Green makes me feel:
At one with nature … especially when I see the tall cottonwood trees in full leafy splendor and there is tall grass that's wet from the dew and my jeans get wet to the knees. I'm so grateful to be alive and at one in nature. This is where I came to hike the day I learned that you died. I needed and wanted to feel alive and yet it was crushing, this weight of aloneness of being alive in a world without you. It's hard for me to go back there sometimes be-

cause I associate it now with both Mom's death and yours. Mom and I had our last telephone conversation while I was hiking at the lake … and I went there for solace the day I learned you had died. I literally ran there. I just put clothes on, got in the car and drove straight there. I couldn't be inside the house one minute longer. I had to be at the lake with my trees and pelicans and birds … and God. And there were hundreds of heart shaped rocks on the path that day. Never before were there that many and never since. They were from you. And Mom and Grandma. And God. They were my sign from you that you were okay. And each one was nearly perfect. Not the impressionistic ones that you teased me about. "How is that a heart shape?"

Sounds

sounds
carry through the woods
this far

the echo lingers
in the crystalline air
reverberating there

tugging at a memory
from decades past
from a lifetime ago, truly

a soft, insistent purring
hovering in the air
or in my mind's eye

do I remember it
for real, or was it just
a memory of a photo

the softness of a stuffed cat
against my cheek on a long-ago
Christmas morning

pretending
I could feel it purring
against me

wanting a cat
so much that year
every year

my heart
was born
to love a cat

so much I even
pretended to be one
for years on end

curling up
on my cat-shaped rug
at kindergarten nap time

crawling on hands and knees
to meow for my milk
and drink with my tongue

my teachers even mentioned
my wanting a cat
at conference time

my mother
well-aware of this longing
tried to meet it with a stuffed cat

but I
wasn't
assuaged

I carried a "stray" home
and claimed it had followed me
feeding it milk from a pie tin

but, alas
its owner claimed it
back from me that same day

my life
can be marked by
the noticeable times

when I
did not have
a cat

childhood
till
fourteen

college
except when I went
home

grad school
when my parents got
a dog

first few months
in DC before George, then Charlie
came home

when Travis was a baby
and Bianca became the
neighborhood attack cat

until Travis was in 6th grade
and begged us for a cat
Tulip, then Timber

the two years
I lived in a condo and couldn't have cats
so they lived with Travis

the two weeks after
Timber died, after Tulip died
and the house was silent

that was the longest
two weeks of my
entire life

Last Night I Dreamt of a Forest

Last night I dreamt of a forest. The trees were fully covered in leaves, the forest floor was thick with moss and fallen leaves. The air was warm and full of moist condensation from the dew that hung in the air. These were the woods that I played in as a girl. I knew them well. Yet they were denser with time and the elements. Looking back, I could just see our house in the distance. Looking up I could catch glimpses of the night sky.

All of a sudden, my dad and I were cross country skiing under a full moon in these same woods. It was so cold that our breath hung before us in little puffs of frozen smoke. As we skied and breathed into the night air, we skied into our very breath. How had I never noticed that before?

A lone dog barked from a yard in the distance. I turned to my dad to comment on it, but he was gone. I called for him, but he had vanished into the night. When I awoke, I had to remind myself that my dad was fine, having just turned 90 last month. I was rattled by the dream and called him soon, just to hear his voice.

I miss those woods. In the dream, I realized that I visit them often, in my mind's eye. When I need to be in the company of green. When I need to breathe that maple-scented air. When I need to feel myself again.

1.2 - Gray - fog / smoke / melancholy

I Slept In Today

I slept in today
not ready to wake
to the day

when light shone through
it was clear
the day had begun

I slipped on my flannel shirt
well yours, truly
and descended

to coffee
to another warm blanket
to light a candle

and
to begin the day
with writing

Expensive

I tried your food
I bought at the vet in the spring
when you were first home

you had rejected it
at first
and I'd had to try another

expensive
buying both wet and dry
for your special UR condition

but you are worth it
I just hate to waste an entire case
of already-bought food

so today
I opened a can and tried it again
you like it, now

eight months later
on your own terms
now that I've been patient

Perhaps

perhaps this is the day
when you will let me
trim your nails

the first week
you were home
you let me, once

then they did
three months ago
at the emergency vet clinic

when you were under
to have a tiny eraser
surgically removed

each other time I've tried
you climb over my shoulder
leaving scratches on my skin

when you make biscuits
your sharp little claws
poke into my legs

so I sit with a blanket
year-round while watching TV
for you to be on my lap

an easy
price to pay
for your adoring love

The New Year is Coming

the New Year is coming
I am not ready
to let go of this one

for this one
held you for nearly half
of it

and yet
the other half held
the deepest chasm of grief I've known

two halves
same coin
love and loss

I am not ready
to let go
of this one

for this one
held another you
for three months

until
you died upon my lap
your fur soft and warm under my hand

my first tears fell
and your fur caught them
as I felt your spirit pass

you grew cold
to my touch and I knew it was time
to let you go

on the day
your ashes returned home
your spirit visited me

through a spectacular light show
of sunshine dancing
on the walls and floor

as your spirit danced
my newly home new cat
played with the light

two halves
same coin
love and loss

miraculously
new cat was here and settled
when the other you left

she comforted me
through both sets of grief
cat and soulmate

just a year
of loss and grief
with a layer of new love

surprising
in a way
that I'm not quite ready

to let this
difficult year go
just yet

but it's also
totally understandable
that it's hard

to let go
the last year
that will ever hold you

I'm stepping into the New Year
tenderly, gently
with no expectations

but if the New Year
can be thought of as gray
that is an improvement over black

the inky jet black of grief
colored over half of this year
with its stain

thinking of walking over
the threshold into even a day of gray
lightens the load considerably

gray is a momentary compromise
one foot in black, the other in white
and my heart mixes them to gray

On Christmas Eve Morning

On Christmas Eve morning
I pulled out my old cell phone
from my top dresser drawer

I walked downstairs
laid it under the Christmas tree
and plugged it in to charge

sitting beneath the tree
I breathed deeply
the pine scent

listening to my mom's messages
saved on this old phone
would be my Christmas gift to myself tomorrow morning

I had done so each year
since she died
this would be the fourth time

each time
and the times in between Christmas
is hard

I feel orphaned anew
realizing deeper each time I hear your voice
there will never be a new message

I have them memorized now
after all the listenings
yet it doesn't get any easier

when you say you love me
when you say don't call you back, it's too hard
when you say you're waiting for my call

all the love in your voice
adds to the love in my heart
yours for me and mine for you

hearing your voice
triggers it all to the surface
from its place just beneath the skin

and for awhile
I'm like the Velveteen Rabbit
tender, bare, exposed

before this Christmas
I've never listened to your messages
with such intention

and this year
there will be another set of messages
to listen to Christmas morning

yours
each one a treasure
calling me Baby, saying "I Love You"

I've listened to this small set
several times in the six months
you've been gone

each time
sobbing deep wracking sobs of loss
of life lived … of life unlived

and the cold realization
that I will never see you again
or hear your voice alive again

and so
I prepare my heart
for this very-different Christmas morning

of waking
to listen to both voices on this old phone
with messages of love, for me

drinking my coffee
with my new cat on my lap
purring to comfort me

of visiting your bench
of bringing you a tiny tree
of tears of grief

for all that has gone
for all that is to be no more
for all the love I've known

and as the world
celebrates the birth of a tiny baby of hope
I do my best

to get through
this first Christmas
without you

life disappears
into the fog
with my heart

fog comes up
from the lake
enveloping all in its wake

you come out of the fog
wholly alive
from the otherworld

Reading

reading
the words on the pages
of your diary

I am there
although it is
an entire century later

you are 13
and I am 62
half a century apart

and
our ages
are reversed

it's as if
I am meeting my grandmother
as a teenager

she was feisty
and funny and we would
have been friends

she had to
remind herself
not to swear

and boy
was she ever
boy crazy

she liked so many boys
in her class that I lost
track of them all

she and my aunt and uncle
loved to go ice skating
and Jack always lost his shoes

she loved her parents
and was very religious
which surprised me

she loved to read
do crossword puzzles
and went to the movies all the time

I hadn't known she'd lived
right in the city when she
was growing up

went swimming in
Lake Michigan all the time
as a girl

her family was very social
with extended family
and friends

meeting my Great Grandma Inglis
when she was at her prime
was also very cool

technology was different
Victrola, the radio
streetcars

she wanted to work at a store
and found and lost several jobs
but proved she could do it

deposited an entire dollar
at the bank on the day after payday
seemed an accomplishment

then one entry
of her meeting my grandfather
entered years later, in pencil

an entire decade
of her diaries missing
the 1930s

what I wouldn't give
to read those entires
from a powerful time

the Great Depression
her marriage
her children born

then I found your love letters
with Grandpa Joe
and copies of your wedding week

and a puzzle piece
slid into place
in my heart

I read two decades
in two days
my mind was swimming

called my dad last night
and shared some memories with him
from your diaries

he loved hearing the stories
illnesses cured
trips taken

we laughed because
he was 10 in the last diary
and 90 now

my mind
was having to fast forward
eight decades

meeting my grandma at 13
and my dad as a boy
is an incredible treat

reading about different
relatives and family friends
being born is surreal

and the deaths
are surreal and sudden
like they were in those times

and sometimes
are still
today

looking up addresses
on mapquest to see
pictures of places today

and finding bxw photos
in my photo boxes
of what was being described

filled in gaps
in my mind
and added to the story

to read
about first times
watching television

and the names
of movies seen at the theater
that I've seen myself

like Desk Set
with Hepburn and Tracy
one of my favorites

as I read throughout
two whole days
I noticed so many similarities

things we enjoyed
patterns to our days
traits I've inherited

and although this is Grandma's story
it is inherently mine
as well

for I began in her
and in my Grandpa Joe
nature and nurture

1.3 - Gold - glittering / richness / abundance

With You On My Lap

with you on my lap
two blankets for warmth
and hot coffee on the end table

I listen to the poems
for inspiration
on this frigid late December morning

my to-do list
on the counter
plans for the day

and yet
hanging in the balance
between years

the sun is also slow to rise
as if saying it is lingering
here this final day of the year

with just a sliver or two
of golden rays
reflected on the wall

bright light
is your sign to me
of greeting

now that you
have passed through the portal
from life to what comes next

my heart
believes its heaven
my mind reflects that hope

and in each ray of sunshine
I feel your love descending
to warm my heart

the only other light
is the golden dots
of fairy lights

still wrapped around
the drying yet still standing
Christmas tree

I always hate
to take it down each year
wanting the light of Christmas to linger longer

this year
will be even harder, still
for the light didn't fully enter in

to this weary
aching heart
filled with loss and grief

this first year
since you left
and only return in the light

and the fourth year
since mom left
and returns with each gingko

and the third year
since Grandma left
and returns with each memory

so much accumulated loss
for this weary, tender heart
to absorb

among the other losses
of marriages and families
no longer alive

two soul-cats
crossing the rainbow ridge on this lap
on this very blanket

that now holds
new love in a new cat
that reminds me

that life and love
truly do
go on

In Reading Your Diaries

in reading your diaries
from when your life was joy
I am meeting you for the first time

when you were young
and everything was happening
for the first time

falling in love
with my grandpa
who died before I was born

I see the love of your life
through your eyes
on the page

and now I am learning
your story from you
22 years after you are gone

what a gift you left behind
for me, for now
just when I need it most

I will learn
how you endured
losing the love of your life

the first Christmas
after I have lost
mine

your diaries
were here all along
these two decades

I just needed to
unpack them from their boxes
open them and begin

and now that I've started
I cannot put them down
one by one, I meet you anew

The Next Time

the next time
which might be today
that I am feeling lonely or bereft

all I need to do
to fill my heart
is read this gratitude list

God
Jesus
the holy spirit

Travis
and Haley
and the pups

Adeline
Tulip
Timber

Todd
and all the love he brought to me
shared with me
still has for me

Julia and Sandy
Dad
Joe

Courtney, Dave, Cody & Alex
Lindsay, Ryan, Ollie & Joy
Mason

being a teacher
and my class
my colleagues

being a writer and having my poems accepted
Beth Kempton for this course and others
the poetry communities I'm a part of

being a painter and having my paintings accepted
the joy of creating
Louise Fletcher

FYJ
and Momentum -
the transformation of my painting

Grief Share group
the people
and the healing

Donna and James
Vera and Del
Bev

all my Michigan friends
Haley's family
the joy of being part of their wedding in May

nature
and the beauty
of living in Colorado

water
my lake, rivers
Lake Michigan

being able to travel
to see Julia and friends in MI
Dad and family in NC

music, books, movies
the memories of all the amazing happy times in my life
the places I've traveled and the longing to travel more

the feeling of learning and teaching new things to my students
the dream of opening an art center in Michigan
volunteering - at church, in the community

having all of my basic needs taken care of
having a family to turn to in times of need
emotionally and otherwise

living in a progressive state
living in a country where
I can protest and have free speech

seeing Christmas lights while driving
and watching Christmas movies
hearing music

going to live music with friends or on my own
having the means to meet my needs and pursue my passions
having passions like writing, painting, reading, traveling

having a team
of health care providers
whom I trust

having faced death
several times and been blessed
to have more life to live

having a place to turn to to work through this accumulative grief
having a great education - growing up, as a young adult, later on
being a lifelong learner

having been born into a family
that values faith and education
and community and family

that Travis and Haley are considering
moving to Illinois, which will be close to Michigan
when I move there in 3 ½ years

Mark - miss teaming with him but grateful for his ongoing friendship
Abigail - grateful for her being my teammate
friendships at CCE - Lori, Rachel, Will, Emily, Stacey, Katie Bell, Liz, Erika, Sara, Devan, Jess
sunlight shining in my eyes right now
Constant Comment tea with a slice of orange
hot coffee every morning

the smell and sound of rain
the smell of fresh bread baking
the feel of Adeline on my lap

summers and weekends off
time to focus on my passions
after school each day

although it can be lonely at times
living alone gives me more time
for pursuing passions

extended family across the country
extended family here - taco lunches now and then
time with friends to talk and catch up

overall, my health
having been raised by a mom and dad who loved me
having my grandparents, aunts and uncles, cousins be a wide-
reaching net of family

feeling like something bigger than myself
in choirs and musicals
playing the piano - and Phyllis Frisbie

connections with former students who come back - summers
connections with former teachers whom I still see
Christmas cards from people throughout my life

the anticipation of next books being published
the anticipation of having 30 ish books out for consideration
the feeling each new month of flipping my poetry and submitting
anew

having gone to school at great schools - and staying in touch with HS friends in michigan
powerful connections of longtime friends - like Julia - and the powerful connections of newer friends - liza & kids, sandy, donna & james, sky & family, bev, grief share, cog,

God puts friends in my path just when I need them

1.4 Blue - Sea, Sky, Vastness

The Taste of Blue

surprises of blue
throughout my day
warming me through

the sunlight
shining against your ebony fur
turning it blue-silver in places

your half of the closet
against Dad's brown half
your favorite color

your eyes
my eyes
connecting us

truth
wisdom
calm

creativity
knowledge
peace

all the colors
known and unnamed
between purple and green

the color of morning
day
and evening

and also
the color of the dark of night
hidden inside the ebony sky

folded inside
of a cloudy sky
on the other side of rain

on the surface
of every body of water
reflecting the sky

not an accident
that the TARDIS
is blue

taking us on adventures
through time, space
introducing us to ourselves

my favorite
genre of music
the blues

interesting how
it is in the plural form
for one blue unravels another

the cumulative experience of loss
grief and sadness knows grief and sadness
the spiral of loneliness

why is there something blue
in every new wedding
to remind us of the bitter with the sweet

the sky expands overhead
the sea stretches out to the horizon
blue connects us to the universe

blue
as cold as an iceberg
as warm as a sunny day

and every
single temperature
in between

how can blue be
the taste of sadness and
the flavor of hope simultaneously

the shades of blue
are as infinite
as the drops in the ocean

periwinkle
the color of adventure and
that favorite crayon out of 64

powder
the color of every single gift bag
at your three baby showers

robin's egg
the delicate shell beneath the nest
when you spread your wings

light
the color of ducks on your favorite blanket
sadly left at a hotel on a road trip back home

royal
the shutters on our first house
the colors of independence and dreams coming true

Dodge Dart
the color of my first car
white vinyl roof

TARDIS
the box that is bigger on the inside
and steals my heart every episode

cyan
your favorite color
even at nine, sophisticated

turquoise
my favorite color paint
when painting … anything

navy
the color of elegance
alongside black

midnight
the backdrop for every night sky event
filled with wishable shooting stars

sky
I fall up
into you

sea
mesmerizing waves
I can see forever

electric
don't touch it, don't even look at it
Spinal Tap, Andrea

sapphire
my birthstone
September

violet blue
the mix of our favorites
yours and mine

my blue crayon
usually the shortest in the box
at that sky

1.5 - Orange - light / heat / nourishment

I Wake Early

I wake early
even though I've slept in
it is still dark outside

just the edges of dawn
are also rising
with me

I wheel the trash bin out
a day late because of
New Year

and brew a pot of coffee
feeding my insistent cat
her wet foot

and a treat
of pulled chicken
that she now thinks of as her breakfast

I light a candle
gather my journal and pen and chrome book
and wrap myself in a blanket to write

a spark flutters in my heart
when I remember that today
is write-by-candle-light day

I do that every day, now
but started it two years ago
with this same exercise

my cat
having finished breakfast
snuggles into my lap

so my chromebook gets nudged
onto the arm of the sofa
at an awkward, yet still do-able, angle

she already knows the voice
of my writing coach
and it's her signal to snuggle

today's color is orange
and I've already written several poems
during the morning spark

and now we've done the meditation
of staring into candlelight
and the backs of our eyes

and I am ready
to share what
spoke to me

Candlelight Dances

the candlelight dances
there are two wicks in this this candle
both dancing

thin lines of light
reflect down and out
from each flame

I think it's my reading glasses
causing the reflection
but it's magical, nonetheless

and as I close my eyes
per the instructions
I'm curious at what I see

as my cat is nudging me
warm and cozy with all her fur and purring
I see a black rectangle hovering before me

it is a small shape
compared to the size of my vision
but it dominates in its darkness

around the vertical rectangle
a halo of light begins to emerge
just at the edges of the ebony

and slowly
almost imperceptibly
the light spreads to fill the space

I simply breathe and observe
noticing what I see
noticing what's happening

as I hear the voice coaching me
I watch as the black rectangle recedes
it becomes further and further away

it doesn't change shape or size
so much as it fades into the distance
and light takes its space

at first I'm focussing
on the darkness fading
but then I see the light

it is soft, diffused
and so gentle
and calm

I am at peace
in this light
that has quietly emerged

to fill the space
that had been dominated
by the dark

and when the gong sounds
and it is time to open my eyes
the light is there, too

and in my cat's purring
and in the candle flame dancing
and in the fairy lights on the tree

there is gentle light around me
there to quietly, calmly
wake the day with me

You Look At Me Differently

you look at me differently
when I wear
my reading glasses

you stare into my eyes
deeply
intentionally

I wonder if
you're just seeing your own
reflection

1.6 - Silver - moonlight / mystery / illusion

I Woke

I woke with the notion
I want to write
this morning

lighting my candle
pine scented for the season
I look up

the full moon
round in its perfection
resonates in its luminescence

silver against the predawn night sky
framed in the tiny window above
my patio sliding glass door

my heart stirred
and with coffee in hand
I nestled on the couch to write

opening the day's prompt
I saw the color silver
and smiled

silver
the fancy-pants name
for gray

gray with a sparkle
of fairy dust-meets magic
silver

silver
sounds so much prettier than
gray

we were graying
when we first met
but went silver together

tinfoil hand-cut stars
a bit of glitter still clinging to them
first decoration every year

just a glimpse
of the silver full moon
I am whole

Moving Aside

moving aside
my reluctant cat
nestled comfortably on my lap

I rise
to open the curtains
to the day

the light has been
trying to peak through the shutters
to wake me

gold competing
with the gray of the dawn
creating a silver shimmer

this is the moment
that begins my day
you in the light

calling me
toward the light
toward the day

the gentle positivity
makes my heart flutter
with memory, with possibility

in the juncture
of what has gone before
and what lies ahead

Silver Is

silver is
so many things
when I stop to consider

the tinfoil stars
cut out by our hands
decades ago

reminding me
of childhood wonder
and enduring love

silver is
the color
of remembering

the sheen of chrome
on our Harley
taking us up the canyon

me holding on tight
and letting go
simultaneously

silver
is the color
of adventure

the buckle of your collar
that lies atop
your box of ashes

next to your pawprint
and a tuft of fur still soft
and warm

silver
is the color
of love

your wedding ring
tapped silver in a thick band
still holds the shape of you

now worn
on my hand
instead of mine

silver
is the color
of forever

the spiral
of my notebook
that holds my words

in dreamlike form
that morph into poems
and poem-dreams

silver
is the color
of what if

the tiny crane
folded with care
out of a gum wrapper

on the table
at the restaurant
where we met

silver
is the color
of peace

the hand-made cross
you bought me
in Idaho Springs

when we were there
on the bike
one weekend

I wear it
every day
remembering

silver
is the color
of believing

moonlight
reflected in your eyes
showing me eternity

magical
in the wonder
of its halflight

silver
is the color
of the unsaid

the coins
from around the world
shapes and sizes

the silver ones
stand out to me
valuable by their nature

every single time
I am asked to choose gold or silver
I choose silver

silver
is the color
of infinity

The Man With The Silver Hair: A Micro Story in 100 Words

Across from me on the bus is a man with silver hair, reading.

Could his book be *The White Dragon* that you gave me on our first date? The first book you ever read to me. Such adventure and possibility.

More people get on and I join the silver haired man. I see the familiar cover. Locking eyes, it is *you.* I can't breathe. You say: "Looking ahead is far more productive than looking behind." Inexplicably, the man is himself again.

It is my stop. Heeding your words, I step off the bus, carrying the electric moment into the day.

1.7 - Black - darkness / shadow / void

A Study in Black

Black looks like:
my cat, black crayon, ink, night sky, radiator / space heater, coffee, the wheels of my car, pencil lead, black hats, black gloves, leather coat, leather boots, Harley, bandana, sunglasses, black beans, licorice, black and white photos, printed page, newspaper, skid marks on the pavement, skunk, zebra, black horse, Kodiak, truck, black line, shadows, the sky against the moon, black sand, a French beret

Black smells like:
coffee brewing as I walk down the steps in the morning, brewed by someone else. The smell of my grandma's house on Christmas morning.

Black feels like:
My leg swinging over the back of the Harley, my legs wrapping around you, my hands wrapping around you, patting my "I'm set" as your left hand squeezes my left thigh and you start the bike. Black feels like my leather boots, my leather coat, my bandana on a hot summer day as we pull out, you rev the grip and I yell "Woo hoo!" into the heat, into the day, into feeling alive. Black feels like the summer heat coming up from the pavement as we stop at a red light, waiting to ride up the canyon into the cool of the day, above the heat we will leave behind. Black feels like freedom as we careen around each curve, smiling with each new vista that is by now a familiar friend. And as we float down a canyon, arms splayed wide like a bird, balancing the bike between your legs … weightless.
black reminds me
that so much living is held inside
one solid color

1.8 - White - snow / purity / beginnings

A Study in White

White looks like:
snow, cat's fur, sheets, hotel towels, hotel bathrobe, toilet paper, tissues, eggs, flour, sugar, teeth, china, stones, fences, clouds, sky, light bulbs, fairy lights, sheep, wool, horses, radishes, potatoes, beaches, waves, foam, cream, white roses, funerals, babies, piano keys, paper, books, the Beatle's White album, light switches, baseboards, shutters, blank canvas, shells, ceilings, stripes, ice, vanilla ice cream, mint flavored gum, fresh mozzarella cheese, epsom salts, salt, crystals, opals, the moon, stars, planets, the milky way, the white of a page against which all words take their shape

White makes me feel:
clean, fresh, new, pure

White makes me think of:
elegance, crispness, clarity, new beginnings

a tuft of your fur
found after you died
resting, still, in a small jar on my piano

the roof of my ‘70 Dodge Dart
and the sense of freedom starting it gave me
every single time

the bleached skull of a cow
hiding in my classroom cupboard
waiting for the best moment to reveal itself

all the space around you
is white in comparison to your dark
matching your one white whisker

that expression “white hot”
never seems to fit me
white is as cold as ice

the white of a page
against which all words
take their shape

white left on a canvas
between bursts of color
where the eye rests

what defines a paragraph
on a page of text
white space

the effervescence
in every glass of carbonation
white space

the softness
of a rabbits fur
white space

the smoothness
of a sheet on the line
white space

the whites of an eye
giving pause to the colored iris
white space

blue sky dotted with clouds
falling up into you
white space

a drizzle
of cream in my coffee
white space

your smile
that lights up your whole face
white space

a zebra
black on
white space

a circle in the
ebony night sky
white space

a picket fence
around the garden
white space

brand new sneakers
unwrapped on Christmas
white space

cream cheese
under the lox atop my bagel
white space

the dress hangs
in the back of my closet
white space

dove's wings
fluttering with peace in my breast
white space

www.ingramcontent.com/pod-product-compliance
Ingram Content Group UK Ltd.
Pitfield, Milton Keynes, MK11 3LW, UK
UKHW041315190726
13845UKWH00025B/283

9 789363 545441